DATE May 25, 2025   MOOD ● ▾

___

OPEN WRITING SPACE

I remember when I was a nigga, and a proud yet lost nigga I was. I was stuck trying to be the best nigga I could, however, I still couldn't do that right. I looked around at people I considered to be "that nigga," and I always fell short. I know, I know the term 'Nigga" and its terminology is offensive to "Black" people, thus referring to yourself as a "Nigga" degrades you as a person.

The good thing about this is Gen 25:21-23- KJV; which states, " 21 And Isaac intreated the LORD for his wife, because she was barren: and the LORD was intreated of him, and Rebekah his wife conceived. 22 And the children struggled together within her; and she said, If it be so, why am I thus? And she went to enquire of the LORD. 23 And the LORD said unto her,

Two nations are in thy womb, And two manner of people shall be separated from thy bowels; And the one people shall be stronger than the other people; And the elder shall serve the younger.

So, here we know that the Old Testament of the Sword of God (The Bible, his word) was written in Hebrew as well as the New Testament was written in Greek. Thus certain words such as bowels do not mean the same thing as it does in the so-called "English" language.

I recently stated, " bowels in James Strong's Strong Concordance meant flesh," as a means to describe a specific skin tone. However, the Father has led me to dig deeper and provide a more in-depth definition of the Hebrew meaning of the word bowels.

Hebrew's definition of the word bowels according to James Strong's New Expanded Exhaustive Concordance of the Bible: Red Letter Edition defines bowels where found in Gen 25:23 KJV when used to reference man (both female and male) in Hebrew (H.) as the word me'eh (may-ey); which in numbers is 4578.

H. 4578 when referring to man is defined as, the seat of generations.

> → Gen 2:4 KJV- "These are the "Generations" of the heavens and the earth, when they were created. - Generations here means history. So, these/this are/is the history of the heavens and the earth.
> → Gen 5:1 KJV- "In this book of the "Generations" of Adam. In the day that God created man, in the likeness of God made he him." - Generations here means a lineage, family registry, history of those

born to this specific bloodline. So, in this book of the lineage, family registry, bloodline, and or family registry of Adam.

Thus, where it states in Gen 25:23 KJV, "they (the twin brothers) will be separated by their bowels, the Lord is referring to their genealogy. One's genealogy determines the pigment of the flesh said family has; whereas the genealogy of a person determines whether they will have melanated skin or pale skin.

When you understand that a person's genealogy determines their demeanor in every situation you will then understand James Strong's 4578 H. definition of bowels not only in the perspective of men, but in the figurative aspect which defines bowels as the heart.

Thus where it states in Gen 25:23 KJV, "they will be separated by their bowels," the Lord here is figuratively referring to the heart of both brothers. The heart of the eldest twin Esau will differ from the heart of the youngest brother Jacob. A person's heart is tied to their genealogy.

A person who has a generation or family history of violence, malice, unforgiveness, bitterness, deceptiveness, and or murder, will differ from a person who has a generation of long suffering, peace, abundance, love, humility, forgiveness, faith, and or truth. The only exception to a person's heart with a lineage of sin, is if *they were set apart to be the chosen vessel within that lineage.*

The eldest twin's emotions, actions, distress, and love (all things felt from the heart) differs from that of the same from the younger twin, due to the generation of said twin.

Gen 25:25-26 KJV states, " And the first (twin) came out red, all over like a hairy garment; and they called his name Esau." 26 " And After that came his brother out, and his hand took hold on Esau's heel; and his name was called Jacob....."

Gen 27 KJV states, ".....And Esau was a cunning hunter, a man of the field; and Jacob was a plain man, dwelling in tents.

Cunning is mostly referred to in the bible as one who uses manipulation, cleverness and deceit in their ways. Gen 3 KJV depicts Satan as being cunning as he subtly manipulated and deceived Eve.

History teaches us that the generation of man who lived and dwelled in tents were those known as the Native Americans (Plain Indians).

So, based on the Sword of God it is safe to say Jacob the younger twin from Issac and Rebekah is a nation which began with and includes Plain Indians. While Esau was a nation embedded in manipulation, deceitfulness, and negative ways that intertwine its cleverness.

Gen 25:30 KJV- "And Esau said to Jacob, Feed me, I pray thee, with that same red pottage; for I am faint: therefore was his name called Edom, hence the Edomites.

Strong Concordance H. 123 (Edom) from h. 122; red; from h. 119- to show blood in face, i.e. flush or turn rosy:- dyed red.

Thus it is safe to say that the Edomites (Edom) are what America considers the so-called "Caucasians." The Edomites from Edom (a Hebrew term) and Idumea (a Greek term) are from the same region; a region of the mountains. History informs us that Caucasian derives from Caucus, a mountain where people of Edomites genealogy dwelled in caves within the mountains of Mount Seir; formally inhabited by the Horites Gen 14:6, 36:20. Generations tend to remain and or return to regions where their lineage reside; i.e. mountain men, and plain men.

By now a question is probably being asked on the lines of, "Cassandra, what does all of this have to do with the good thing about calling yourself nigga?"

Great question. I am getting to the answer, however, in order for me to answer it I have to go back into history so it can make sense in the present. Follow me and it will all make sense.

Thus far we know that the brothers were separated by their lineage and their heart, as told by God. Even in the womb they fought and struggled to occupy the same womb.

Once you understand James Strong's Concordance definition of H. me'eh 4578 in the perspective of man and figuratively, you will then begin to understand h. 4578 in the plural sense is connected to both the perspective of man and figuratively. Where h. 4578 in the plural sense means intestine. The plural sense is connected because the intestine sits near the uterus, and h. 4578 in the collective sense is defined as the uterus.

The intestine is repositioned in the stomach during the pregnancy of a woman, and the fetus/embryo of the baby grows in the uterus which is also called the womb of a woman.

We should know by now that, womb in the bible, as defined in James Strong's Concordance is h. 7358 (Rachem). Womb which is also called bowels is defined to mean Matrix Exodus 13:15 KJV.

Thus where it states in Gen 25:23 KJV, "they will be separated by their bowels," the Lord here in the plural sense and collectively is referring to the Matrix.

So, they will be separated by their Matrix. Whereas one of the twins would be born by the Spirit of the only living God, and the other would be born into the spirit of the most low, Satan.

Therefore, regardless of what a person says, what a man thinks displays what is in his heart Proverbs 27:3 KJV. Whereas, what is in a man's heart determines the matrix a person is operating in.

Thus where it states in Gen 25:23 KJV, "they will be separated by their bowels," the Lord here is stating, "Esau and Jacob will be separated by not only their lineage and bloodlines, but also the contents of their heart, and said content will not only determine what matrix they live in but also show their character due to the fruit they bear.

There is such a thing as bloodline patterns and bloodline curses. We know bloodline or generational curses are repeated sin that God allows to continue down the bloodline until a chosen vessel breaks the cycle.

A repeated pattern is something that is not necessarily bad but is also found in a person's lineage generation after generation. I use the word generation as the Westernized American definition, not the actual Hebrew definition as told in the bible.

When we look at Abraham, and his generation (Hebrew definition here) we see a specific pattern that God uses within this said generation.

Let us first take a look at Abraham and Sarah. In any marriage arranged or approved by the Most High God there are three strands. The three strands consist of the husband (1), the wife (2), and the Holy Spirit/Ghost (3); where the Holy Ghost is in between the husband and the wife created a three stranded braid (not easily broken).

In Abraham's case his marriage had doubt and fear within it, so it had a three stranded braid, but it was not always braided with the Lord in the middle.

Sarah wanted to conceive a child. However, God pushed back Sarah becoming a mother until she was of old age. Due to such, Sarah became impatient and convinced Abrahman to fornicate with his Egyptian maid Hagar. Ishmael was conceived between Hagar and Abraham. Genesis 16:4 KJV.

Sarah at ninety (90) years finally gave birth to Issac Genesis 21:1-3 KJV.

God already informed Abraham in Genesis 17:19-21 that Ishmael would not be the son he would establish his covenant with, it would be his son Issac born with his wife Sarah. So, when Sarah requested that Abraham force Hagar to leave their home once Issac was born because she caught Ishmael making a mockery out of Isaac in his young age. Genesis 21:8-21 KJV, God in Genesis 21:12 KJV advises Abraham he should follow the instruction of his wife Sarah.

So, here Ishmael was the first born, but the second born Issac received the promise to inherit God's covenant.

The same thing happened in Abraham's generation with Isaac's twin sons. Esau was the first born, however, God informed Isaac in Genesis 25:23 KJVthat the older son (Esau) would serve the younger (Jacob). This establishes that intended for the covenant to continue again with the second born not the first.

This is considered a generational pattern within the Abrahamic lineage.

The generational curse within the Abrahamic covenant began with Abraham lying (a trademark of Satan) to Abimelech about his wife Sarah being his sister Genesis 20:1-16 KJV. Abraham's lie out of fear(the effect of having no covenant with God) of death caused Abimelech to commit adultery by taking another man's wife and marrying her.

Although the covenant between Abraham and God was created (Genesis 15 KJV) that would continue with his lineage, the Satanic traits of fear, and deception already became embedded in the Abrahamic generation.

Again it was revealed in Genesis 25:23 KJV that Esau was to serve Jacob prior to their birth. However, Issac in rebellion which is a form of witchcraft (1 Samuel 15:23 KJV) was stubborn which is as iniquity (state of wickedness, lawlessness, malice, moral perversion mainly towards obeying God's commands), and idolatry (1 Samuel 15:23 KJV) deceived Esau into thinking he would become the heir. Thus, Isaac with Esau schemed to overthrow God's will in acts of iniquity by naming Esau as the heir to receive the Abrahamic covenant. Isaac planned a scheme where Esau would bring Isaac a meal in this blind state and he would give the blessings to Esau this way. God seen through all of this thus allowed Rebekah and Jacob to move forth with their plans to deceive Isaac into giving Jacob the promise.

Remember, Esau was hairy all over. So, Jacob and Rebekah shaved an animal and placed its fur all around Jacob to appear as if Jacob who was not hairy was Esau. From he they presented Jacob to blind Isaac as Esau with meat prepared by Jacob, and Isaac was unknowingly forced to adhere to thus saith the Lord (Genesis 27:1-41 KJV).

Although the word of the Lord went forth, the cycle of deceptiveness passed from Abraham went to Isaac and showed up as rebellion, a form of witchcraft, stubbornness, and idolatry. Isaac idolized Esau and the meat he could provide. This same cycle or curse was

passed to Rebekah through sexually transmitted demons
as she laid with her husband; then it showed its head
again in Jacob when he worked with Rebekah to deceive
Isaac.

From there this deceptive, yet stubborn and rebellious
curse passed down to Esau as an iniquity malice, as he
became evil towards and vowed in his <u>heart</u> to kill his
twin brother Jacob for receiving the blessings wrongfully
promised to Esau, although they were Jacob's to begin
with (Genesis 27:41-46 KJV).

Jacob heard Esau was planning to come and meet with
him, years after being sent away by his parents to save
him from being murdered by Esau; and Jacob was afraid
and feared Esau calling himself Esau's servant (Genesis
32:6-7 KJV).

This began the era of Jacob whose name was changed to
Israel hence the Israelites being afraid of Esau whose
name was changed to Edom hence the Edomites and the
began the era of the Israelites settling for less than the
Father called us to be. The founding father of the Israelites
settled to be inferior to the Edomites, although we were
called to be superior.

The generational curse of Fear that passed from Abraham
fell upon the generation of Jacob/Israel, while on the other
hand the generational curse of giving blessings/rights to a

nation that it did not belong to or that did not deserve it passed from Isaac to Esau/Edom.

The Israelites which began with Plain Indians, later to included several Hispanic/Latin/Spanish cultured groups, Hati, the so-called African Americans, the lists goes on used The Heavenly Father to beat the children of Seir, then turned around and began idolizing serving, and bowing down to the gods of the children of Seir which are the Edomites (2 Chronicles 25:14 KJV).

Submitting to the gods of the nation who vowed to kill us automatically renders us inferior and submissive to that nation.

When you begin worshiping a specific nation, person, deity, or thing, you forge a covenant with everything that person stands for regardless if you fully agree to it or not and you come into agreement with the laws and regulations of said covenant.

When the children of my founding fathers Abraham, Isaac, and Jacob/Israel began the covenant to worship the god of the children of Seir they no longer walked in the image as our Heavenly Father viewed us in. The Israelites began walking in the image as the gods of the Edomites viewed us as.

When it comes to me and the classification I was given as African American which is really the Tribe of Judah, the same tribe as Yeshua, once my generation yielded to the gods of the Edomites and it passed to me; I became what they wanted me to be viewed as and view myself how they wanted me to view myself, which is/was a nigga.

The difference between the Israelites when Jacob roamed the earth was they did not have the law of the spirit of Yeshua, thus fell victim to being condemned by the spirit of the flesh. The law of the Spirit of life in Yeshua has made us free from the law of sin and death (Romans 8:1-2 KJV).

So, in retrospect the absence of a covenant with the Most High God is the beginning of a covenant with another god.

Ishmael, the first born of Abraham became the father of the Ishmaelites, and he bore 12 sons who became the 12 princes of Allah. The story of Hager and Ishmael is not in the bible referencing Yeshua, because that bible is solely for the history of Yeshua. The Quran which I have not read speaks of the story of Hagar and Ishamel. Where the story ends in the bible of Yeshua regarding Hagar and Ishamel, is where the story begins in the Quran regarding Hagar and Ishamel being founders of the Islamic nation.

Once Sarah died, Abraham remarried a woman named Keturah, after he found Isaac a wife and had six more sons named,: Zimran, Jokshan, Medan, Midian, Ishbak, and Shuah. These sons were sent away by Abraham to

protect Isaac as being the heir to the Abrahamic covenant,
but they were sent away with gifts. These sons later
became a part of different Arab nations apart from
Ishmael.

The difference between every nation being sent away with
something and Edom being sent away with nothing is
every other nation I mentioned came from Abraham, who
already had a covenant with the Most High God, and
Esau worked to go against God's plan for Jacob to be the
heir. Then Esau hated God's elect to the point where he
vowed to kill him.

The heart of Edom here differs from the heart of Israel
here today, and the hate from Edom to Israel as well as
the submissiveness and the spirit of inferiority displayed
by Israel towards Edom.

I have said this once and I will say it again, there is no
such thing as free will within our lives. The only free will
we have is to choose to serve The Most High God, smaller
gods, or the most low god who is Satan.

The difference between the Arab gods, Islamic gods, and
the most low god Satan, is the Arab gods and the Islamic
gods do not set out to come against The Most High God,
they just were not granted the opportunity to have a
covenant with the Most High, so their people, (though hell
bound if they do not believe in Yeshua) believe in different
principles and policies, whereas the most low god Satan, is

a fallen angel, he started with the Most High God,; he knows better, he copies God, he is in competition with God (although God is not competing back, because you cannot compete where there is no comparison), and he is literally coming against God's people as we work to stop him, and set the captives Satan has caught free.

This too is why you may see many Natives, so called Blacks, and Hispanics members of Islamic religions and nations, and even more within the Satanic nation of Edom. Just because the Israelites were given the covenant, does not mean we have to take it. We have to make the only free will choice we have, and that is to decide whether you serve God or the devil. Even the Islamic and Arab, or Catholic religions fall under the category of choosing Satan, because the Sword of God states, "if you do not keep the commandments, or accept Yeshua as Lord and Savior you hate the Lord." If you hate the Lord you fall under the god of Edom. If you do any acts that go against the Most High God, you fall under the god of Edom. The nation you were born in does not matter, the god you chose to serve is the only thing that matters. You can be from the Nation of Islam and believe then confess out of your mouth Yeshua is Lord and you will be saved.

The Islamic version of what happened between Hagar and Ishmael could very well be true, keep that truth and knowledge, but confess out of your mouth that Yeshua is Lord, keep the commandments of the Father and be saved.

God said Ishmael would be a father of a nation, this is true, he was the father of Islam, now keep that truth and confess that Yeshua is King, and be saved. Acknowledge that The God of Abraham, Isaac and Jacob/Israel gave his covenant to Jacob, protected Ishamel in the wilderness upon stumbling on to Islam, keep the principles you have learned through Islam so long as they do not conflict, or go against the God of Abraham, confess that Yeshua is the Messiah, and rose of the third day, keep the commandments of the God of Abraham and be saved. The God of Abraham blessed his son Ishmael and his descendants promising they would be a great nation and they are. Now that this is established, now believe and confess that Yeshua is King of the 12 princes of Islam and is Lord and be saved.

Yes, Ishmael is the founder of Islam and his 12 sons are the 12 princes of Islam. Yes Jacob/Israel is Ishmael's younger brother the founder of the Israelites, his 12 sons form the 12 tribes of Israel. Ishmaelites/Islam, you believe in Yeshua but just as a messenger. I implore you to fast with true followers of Yeshua, to pray with true followers of Yeshua, so that the correction can be made that Yeshua was not just a messenger but the Messiah. From here, I implore you to believe then confess out of your mouth that Yeshua is king and join the team of salvation.

The Nation of Islam, and the Nation of Israel under the belief that Yeshua is our Lord and Savior is and will be a beautiful thing.

However, I digress.

The Spirit of God helps us in our infirmities, we do not know what to pray for or how to pray, so the Spirit itself intercedes for us providing the discernment on what to pray for; And he that searches the <u>hearts</u> knows what is in the minds of the adopted children of God, because the Spirit maketh intercession for the saints according to the will of God (Romans 8:26-27 KJV).

The aforementioned is proof that the only free will we have in our life is the free will to choose Satan or the Most High God. The thoughts, ideas, visions, desires, likes, dislikes, spirits, and loves, are placed within our hearts, and minds by the God we choose to follow as they intercede on our behalf; according to the desires of that specific god's heart.

When you fall into sin, and or whore after other gods and make idols, Satan, the fallen angel/ devil and his desires are what you think and become. If you have a generation of sin then the bloodline curse passed down to visit the third and fourth generation will find you and you will continue the cycle of bondage until the chosen vessel breaks the chains of bondage off of those yearning to and willing to follow the Most High God.

My blood family did not fully understand who God was, so they could not teach me to love what was in me because they did not operate with the spirit that was in me. So, they taught me how to hate myself. I didn't think like them. Edom's educational system couldn't brainwash me, so I didn't test like them. I didn't like what those in the world liked, so I wasn't accepted like them. I was set apart but no one told me the value I had within me; so I was set apart and I didn't want to be. I wanted to be what Edom classified everyone who bought into their matrix was. I wanted to be a nigga, but I could not nigga right. Edom recognized me as a threat early on, and labeled me a trouble maker within my family, a liar within the streets, mentally unstable to those who offended me.

I wanted to be a nigga but the system that Edomites created for niggas rejected me. I was a reject, I was a rebel. However, this time I was a rebel with a cause, and the cause was I was chosen. I was chosen not to conform with the system, but to destroy the system. In the words of my Islamic historian Malcolm X, "One does not conform to the system, they destroy it."

Many scholars have referred to the term "nigga," equivalent to that of an ignorant person, where ignorant means a lack of knowledge. This theory has been deemed inaccurate, but I beg to differ.

Hosea 4:6 KJV states, "My people are destroyed for a lack of knowledge." Ignorance displays a lack of knowledge; and to be a nigga, an Israelite has to first confrom to the matrix of the Edomites. Conforming to the matrix of the Edomites while truly being an Israelite is a form of ignorance. The only was an Israelite can be a nigga is they have to first operate in the same fear and inferiority Jacob/Israel did when he learned Esau/Edom was looking for him. One must adapt the spirit of fear of their enemy, and said fear causes them to be a servant to the oppressor who seeks out to oppress you.

To conform to the matrix of Edom as an Israelite of any other nation means, said nation will no longer be separated by the bowels with Edom.

Bowels in Hebrew again means me'eh 4578 where bowels is defined in four different aspects:

1. The generation of man- where the bloodline and the trials and tribulations of the bloodline differ
2. Figuratively - how the heart of the bloodline loves, acts towards others, shows compassion, shares wealth, etc
3. In the plural sense- where the organs that surround the womb affect the development of the baby.
4. Then collectively- the womb/ which is the uterus and means matrix holds the baby, and the aforementioned determines what matrix the baby will be born into.

When a person of that person's bloodline chooses to follow the gods of Edom, the children they have or they become a product of the hate Edom has towards Israel. Due to this, they hate their appearance and aim to get surgery altering their looks and self, they hate, have less compassion towards and mistrusts anyone who looks like them only trusting Edomites and those who resemble Edom. While pregnant, the majority of women experience abuse during the pregnancy whether it's physical, mental, emotional, drug/ alcohol, or eating abuse, which affects the intestine surrounding the uterus, and plays a part in the babies development. From here, the abuse, the heart posture, the bloodline before the pregnancy and its god determines the matrix the next generation is born into.

My parents were involved in sexual perversion which includes childhood molestation/rape, fornication (premartial sex), porn watching, homosexuality, sexual orgies, sex with animals, molesting and or raping while in adulthood, adultery, etc. Not saying they did all of these acts, but they did some of them. My parents had unforgiveness, deceptiveness, to name the least. Neither of my parents fasted to break this curse from falling to me, or fully accepted Yeshua to save me, so the curse fell upon me, and I had no idea.

So yes, I was born a nigga within Satan's matrix and I would soon hate myself and be influence to open myself up to more demons through the spirit of sexual perversion by fornicating why not married.

Let's talk about the sexual perversion in my life . My first crush in elementary school was my older male cousin. The obsession was real. This is not the era of Jacob, we do not marry our cousins. That is trifling. Thank God he healed me from that early.

I would make poems and raps about fornicating when I got older as a virgin. The desire I had to fornicate so the generational cycle of premarital sex and teen pregnancy could continue through me was unreal. I talked a real good game. While a virgin I was a lioness with my back down ready to pounce on the dick. When I lost my virginity I became a kitten with my back up ready to bounce from the dick. I couldn't take or hold dick like a gambler can't hold credit.

I thought it was my mother who first me to get an abortion when I became a pregnant teen, but it was the demons familiar with the bloodline using my first baby as a sacrifice to molech to further, and deepen the demonic hold on my bloodline through me.

The key was to get me to settle with the low level life I was leading, and I did early on. I had no guidance. I wasn't as versed in the covenant as the rest of those in my family. I was set apart from my family, I did not act like anyone else in my family. I couldn't represent the bloodline covenant right. I was disqualified to be in my family.

I thought I was not good enough for sexual perversion. I didn't understand and was not taught who I was in Israel, so I was becoming what the nation we were scattered in wanted me to be. I was becoming a nigga, and a ignorant I was becoming.

I had the heart of God but the mentality of an ignorant nigga. I was trying to mix the heart of God into and with the devil's playground, and I was being taken advantage of, and run over. A house divided cannot stand (Mark 3:25 KJV). I wasn't standing tall in my ignorance, I was falling for everything not too outrageous. I was a people pleasing gofer, I would go for anything.

When it came to sexual perversion and me I had no control. Some of the guys I fornicated with I did not want to, I was bound to the demon that was over the sexual perversion in my bloodline. I was too afraid to say no, and the spirit of fear came from Satan. I was attracted to and felt magnetic connections to be I would never talk to on my worst day, and people I would never find attractive. I settled for what the demon controlling me wanted me to have, which was the lowest of the low. The people the demons who bound me had me around would have led me to an early death.

I had no control over the demons that were operating through me. It is like when a person is high or drunk; they can't control their behavior or actions the same as they can when they are sober. It is the same way when a demon has you bound. They control your moods, your actions, your thought patterns and your behavior. The demon has you bound.

I realised the males in my family carried the same spirits as the men I dealt with outside of my family. So, either way I would be made to feel less than by one or the other. I was abused by one and made to feel less than by the other or a mixture of both by both sides. I was silenced either way. That was the ultimate end game.

Both sinners and saint's lives look the same outwardly at one point. The difference is the bowels that separate them. One could be accepted in and gravitate to a nation that they were not born in and lead their life according to the nation they chose to exist in.

Sexual perversion was the biggest generational curse I was bound to and had to overcome. I was molested, I was raped, and I fornicated out of marriage be it while bound by demons or when I yielded to the call of Satan pulling through the generational curse he has placed within my family years ago. Growing up with my parents I always lived in areas where demons had dominion.

For example: passing billboards promoting Planned Parenthood, where babies are aborted thus sacrificed to Molech. This promotes murder, and human sacrifice. Sex stores promote the spirit of lust, and sexual immorality and perversion. Masonic temples promote demonic idol worship. Getting drunk, or doing drugs from liquor and spirit stores, and weed stores promotes idle minds and ways to open portals to the demonic realm. They call it liquor and spirits for a reason; when you get drunk you open yourself up to the spirits attached to that specific drink. Strip clubs, and tittie bars both promote the spirit of lust. Psychic reading billboards and stores, promotes the spirit of divination and witchcraft. Whenever you see things like this in areas you will see what demon has dominion over that specific region.

These areas are normally low income poverty areas, or high crime areas, and areas that have unfinished and run down homes, businesses, and buildings. You will see drug addicts, prostitutes, drug dealers, panhandlers, children roaming the streets without parents, gang members, and other things of this nature. Satan cannot be everywhere like our living God can, so he has to use the angels who fell with him and the other demons he terrorizes people with to set up shop in different regions so he can be prevalent in different areas at once, and so demonic spirits can roam around those areas; tempting people to sin.

Just because houses are cheaper does not mean you should move there, unless God calls you to that region.

Satan's matrix and the government officials that operate in demonic practices, the businesses and organizations that fund them and other high ranking individuals in demonic occult practices place these types of businesses in these areas to not only keep sin going, but to gatekeep, become rich off of and control those who are controlled by these types of influences.

These types of things are the things that oppress God's people, and those in spiritual wickedness get rich off of the very thing sent to oppress us. This is a generational curse, or a curse from living a life of sin Deuteronomy 28:43 KJV. They hate us, so they keep us in poverty, but get rich off of us.

Let's not forget about the artist singing and or rapping songs that promote sin. They are demonically possessed, so when they are singing these songs they are reciting curses and singing to the demon that possesses them. Thus when we sing these songs we in turn cast spells over ourselves and open demonic portals for the demons that are behind these songs.

Hidden traps designed for my death were orchestrated by family members who secretly hated me. They knew I was destined for greatness, I just didn't know.

The same cousin I visited in Florida while pregnant with my only son, is the same cousin who cursed my kingdom, spouse and my connection. As soon as I told her about him, soon after he ghosted me. I did not hear from him until the next year, and even then it was fragmented. He was there then he would disappear. This is the same cousin who was in my ear, just like the Edomites, telling me "those who stole my son to keep him, as it was the "best thing for my son." All this was part of a destiny transfer, and curses designed to end me. Children are gifts from God and they represent purpose. My son being stolen from me signifies a purpose being stolen. It makes sense now why I would have dreams of people trying to kill me, or me being hunted and right before I died I woke up. This is the spiritual realm alerting me of the destiny swap attempt on my left.

For years my purpose and gifts set dormant while I lived a life of sin and continued the generational curses from both my mother's and my father's side. A purpose unfulfilled, and a life where I always felt void of something I had no clue was missing. Is this life, or there's got to be more to life than this, I always thought.

Even before my purpose being stolen through the human trafficking of my son there were several attempts on my life that Satan, my enemy, meant to end in my death. But God. Someone somewhere hiding their true intentions hiding in the shadows must have been sending up prayers for my protection, because although the weapons formed and I was grazed, they did not prosper. It could have even been God himself alone interceding for me. The attacks missed me but continued down to my children due to my disobedience and nigga behavior.

When my mom pushed me to California I was almost human trafficked, that missed me but fell onto my son. Makes me wonder who else in my bloodline was human trafficked for that to keep cycling around??

I literally triggered the demons in people passed down to them via generational curses, and they had no idea why they did not like and or were jealous of me. This stems back to grade school years.

If I didn't break the cycle the same dark forces that worked to take me out would have surely taken my children out, and at one point I began to see the cycles manifesting. The speed that it began happening to my children was at the rated speed of the current times.

For example, I was hit by a car at seven (7) years old, one of my daughters was almost hit twice younger than five years old.

I was almost human trafficked at 18 years old, my son was human trafficked at birth and there were two human traffic attempts on the same daughter that was almost hit by a car before the age of five. Someone at two different parks within days a part attempted to lure my daughter away. The first attempt was a Spanish girl who did not speak English, and the second attempt the very next day was a young adult male going in and out of the woods next to two of my daughters while gazing at them and circling around them. The next attempt was stopped by God himself. It was a different daughter than the aforementioned and we were at a different park on a different side of town than the first two different parks, and I received a vision that the group of young girls surrounding all of my daughters at the time would jump my oldest daughter then run off with one of my youngest daughters.

An alarm from the pool area went off via an act of God and I was able to call my daughters to return back to me prior to anything transpiring. Once my daughters were back with me, my oldest informed me, "one of the girls kept standing behind her then running off and whispering to her group of friends while staring at my daughter as they huddled together." She informed me also that, "the same girl smiled at the daughter that was almost hit by the car, but that same daughter was in a defensive stance and questioned why she kept standing behind my oldest." My youngest daughter sensed something as well because she clung to my oldest daughter like glue.

These were just the attempts to kidnap my children. When I only had my oldest daughter and no other child, the leasing office in one of the apartments I stayed in lied to the police and told them I left my daughter home alone and at least six squad cars came to my home questioning me. Another attempt happened when my oldest daughter was 11 years old. I went to drop medical paperwork off at the obgyn and someone from a surrounding company called the police and told them I had left small children in the car for up to two hours alone when in actuality it was five minutes. Multiple squad cars appeared, and realized my twelve (12) year old was in the car with my four year old and two year old while they ate their food and watched their tablets and they could not do anything.

So, it is safe to say that Satan is after my children, my purpose. My only son is already gone, and it has been an uphill battle getting him home. I am going up against spiritual wickedness in high places and their hearts are more harden than Pharaoh's was when he refused to let the Hebrews go at Moses's command. He turned ten (10) years old this year and I still do not have him home to date in the physical realm.

I had a spirit of suicide over my life where I would mildly cut and attempt to ingest pills, my oldest daughter drank bleach. Though it was not enough to do any real damage, she too had the same spirit of death/suicide on her life as well. She even put jumping ropes around her neck while staying over a classmate's house where rope burns were

*left around her neck. I still don't know what actually
went on at that sleepover.*

*I was attacked while at one of my mother's family friends'
house by their daughter in Kansas City, my oldest
daughter was beaten by two adults that babysat her. She
told me years later and that made me feel powerless as I
was not able to reach out to the people who hurt my
daughter and I was not able to protect her from that
attack.*

*I was molested and called a liar, and so was my oldest
daughter.*

*My head was bruised and cracked open at seven while I
was hit by a car, one of my youngest daughter's face was
broken due to a fall at an arcade before she turned two
years old. I had a scar in my head, this same daughter has
a scar in the back of her head as I did.*

*I was burned on the arm at the age of one in the second
degree. All of my daughters were burned by an object
flying from the fireplace as we burned things that
connected to someone sent by Satan to kill us.*

*The same things that Satan used against my life were
passed down to my children as I lived a life of sin. Even
being married to the wrong people continued generational
curses. One of my husbands planned to rape my oldest
daughter, and had already began revealing his private*

parts to her and my other daughters as well. I did not witness this, but once I broke the chain of bondage it was revealed to me that he had done this. He would have continued the sexual abuse from me to them. There were times where he would fornicate with me although I told him I did not want to lay around with him. This too is also considered rape regardless of if we were married or not.

I am a recovering sinner. I am not qualified because of my works. I am unqualified made qualified through God's hand. Saul killed God's people in the bible, but God qualified him, changed his name to Paul, and he became an extreme influence for the house of the Lord Acts 13:9 KJV Acts 26:10 KJV. God did not come for the upright, he came to save the lost.

This one may hurt, but I did not come to bring comfort; I came but to bring truth. One seeking the truth should and shall find comfort when they hear it.

Revelation 1:8 kjv, " I am the Alpha and omega, the beginning and the ending saith the Lord, which is and which was, and which is to come, the Almighty."

Here God established that he is the Alpha and Omega, the beginning and the ending. He did not say he was the first of the Alphas and the Omegas, he said he was the Alpha and Omega, so all the Fraternities and Sororities claiming to be Alpha and Omega are blasphemes before God. You *cannot be what God is. You can try to imitate as Satan does, but you can NEVER be what and who God is.*

Let that sink in as you realized the Civil Rights activists you were taught and conditioned to praise growing up were agents of Satan. They had flattering lips and words, but ultimately went against God's will for us. They claimed to be gods by claiming what God is and they led us further into captivity towards those who were sent to oppress us.

They told us we were meant to be equal like all the other nations, but God told us we were above ALL nations on the earth as we were his people. Deuteronomy 14:2 KJV- They stripped us and did a destiny swap of our birthright, then trained and conditioned us to be niggas; and to serve them while they were meant to serve God and the chosen people of God.

They told us to love all and all the things of the world, when God told us. " Do not love the world or the things in the world, and if anyone loves the world, the love of the Father is not in him." 1 John 2:15 KJV.- They conditioned us to hate the ways of God and love the way of Satan to be accepted in their matrix.

The conditioned us to accept abuse, to settle for less than we are while still trying to be equal to those who oppressed us; although God says in Deuteronomy 28:33, "The fruit of thy land, and thy labours, shall a nation

which thou knowest not eat up; and thou shalt be only
oppressed and crushed always." - This is a curse from
sinning against God. They pushed us to be content in
staying in generational curses of disobedience by
conditioning us to believe this was acceptable living.

They conditioned us to believe that love is love and pride
is the acceptance of all love, when God told us in Proverbs
16:18 KJV that, "Pride goeth before destruction, and an
haughty spirit before a fall.- Haughty feeling superior to
others including God and his word, being arrogant. All
love is not Love, some love is a sign of sexual perversion
and witchcraft being in that person's bloodline.

They pushed narratives that brought forth hate, division,
and violence in some cases, and we were conditioned to
believe this is the life God made for us.

They were and are puppets for Satan assigned by Satan to
keep God's people lost, ignorant, and void of the power
they possess when they operate in their birthright; which
is when they operate in the light of God through full
surrender of God's will.

Some of them die violently, are abused in old age, are
nasty, spirited, mean, money oriented, operators of
division, separating God's will from the way of the world,
all in which carry the trademark of Satan.

It does not matter if it sounded or sounds good. Nor does it matter if it appears to give certain people status within a world that rejects them, it's all puppetry, and Satan is the puppet master.

Masons end their prayers with saying, "mote it be," this is strictly Satanic language. Satanists use this phrase in their homage to Satan and in their spells. In the Eastern Star prayer they pledge allegiance to something outside of God just as the frats and sororities do.

These are all organizations and orders of Satan. They are our politicians, senators, entertainers, athletes, actors, civil activists, known pastors, known lawyers, historical figures, heroes, millionaires, musicians, poets. Etc. Murals are being made for them and they are further from God than Satan.

They have created systems and empires that continue God's people in the curses displayed in Deuteronomy. They do not teach us how to break chains of bondage, they create division, hate, and keep us inferior, when God's people beginning with the Plain Indians, were made superior.

In 1776 the Continental Congress adopted the Declaration of Independence on July 4th- This was the beginning of the Revolutionary War and the birth of the United States of America, Satan's Matrix. This was 249 years ago.

An Empire lasts 250 years. In 2026 a new Empire will be forged. This Empire will bring back the tariffs fought against during the civil war, homelessness, less food, less jobs, robots taking over, forced military drafts, God's people (Mexicans, Cubans, Colombians, etc.) being forced out, more hate, starvation, war within the streets, more man made diseases, the lists goes on.

You do not have that much time, what you accept now within this new empire will affect your family for decades to come. It will determine your heart's posture and which God you serve. You will not be provided grace because God has given you decades of grace. You will be locked in to what side you choose.

If you read my previous books you know that zodiac is a death sentence, yoga is a death sentence, fornication outside of marriage is a death sentence, witchcraft and any other form of divination (tarot readings, mediums, physic readings, ancestral worship, horoscopes, star worship, etc.) is a death sentence.

You cannot serve two masters Matthew 6:24 KJV. Either you love the world or you love God. You cannot idol Beyonce and follow God. You cannot have a sneaky freaky link that you have sex with outside of marriage when you are bored, and serve God. You cannot be a Capicorn, Leo, Gemini, Aquarius, Sagittarius, Pisces, Cancer, Virgo, Aries, etc., and serve God. You cannot be a member of a Satanic organization (Mason, Eastern Star, Jehovah

Witness WatchTower), Fraternity, or Sorority and serve God. You cannot idol this made up race system (Black love, Black Power, Black Lives Matter, White Power, etc.) and serve God. You cannot idol worship entertainers, and or yourself calling yourselves High Priestess, High Priest,, Gods and Goddess and serve God.

You cannot straddle the fence. You cannot ride two horses with one butt. You cannot see sin and dwell in its company 2 Corinthians 6:14 KJV. You cannot remain silent when sin is dominating or you are just as guilty. As Marcus Rogers once said, "Casual Christians will be casualties." I am not saying profess to be a Christian, because that too is a religion. However, yes surrender to Yeshua and the Most High.

You have to be all the way Hot for the Father, the Son and the Holy Ghost. Revelation 3:15-16- I know thy works, that thou art neither cold nor hot: I would wert cold or hot. 16 So then because thou art lukewarm, and neither cold nor hot, I will spue thee out of my mouth.

You cannot be against murder but yield to homosexuality. You cannot be against women being abused, but okay with not helping the poor. You cannot be double minded.

Man did I suffer from double mindedness many years in my life. This matrix will condition you to be double minded. Aye, what can I say, I am a recovering sinner.

These politicians, presidents, entertainers, civil activists, athletes, etc., will paint a pretty picture of double mindedness and lead you straight to hell with it. You have to come out of the world and be set apart. You have to renounce and denounce all covenants with the world. The L in the word world signifies God's lost people. Remove the L from world, then pick up what is left, which is the word. Drop the world and pick up your sword which is the word of God. You don't have much time.

The sad part is many will not make it. They will choose the L and remain lost. They will remain the L and blend in with the world and continue to enhance Satan's matrix.

Yes I was in bondage to sexual perversion, I was molested, I was raped, I fornicated outside of marriage, to married people, and I did not speak up when men I would NEVER give a chance forced sex on me. I let them violate my body and remained silent. I was chained to Satan's control. I did not have a voice, so when he wanted these demons to fill me up with demons through sex and silence the voice of God in my life he would control my strength, my mood, and my will, and bind me to having sex with the demons in the lives of those he sent to destroy and take mine.

It's not the sexual, mental, or physical abuse that was the most difficult. It was the process I endured with no father as a security net, no mother to nurture my war wounds, and no friends to encourage me and tell me that what I was doing mattered; and that they were proud of me.

The silent pain and torture that no doctor can write a diagnosis or prescribe medicine for. The silent cries that are unnoticed and hidden because the next day, the next hour, the next minute, the next second, you have to wear a smile because the grind does not stop when you feel defeated; and the hustle will not wait for you to pull yourself together, and find your balance.

You give your all to uplift others while giving nothing to yourself and receiving nothing from others because you have no support system.

You have to dim your light in certain places or the opposition gets jelly and says you're doing too much, or you are too serious, and you have no chill. But how can you chill?

Chilling is not a luxury for you and you did not choose this struggle, it chose you. You do not have the system those jealous of you have, and if you fall apart for a second you will be labeled as unstable.

So you are stuck in the fire, in the middle of the flames.

On the left side of the fire they pressure you to dim your light. On the right side if you slip up just a little, they will label you unstable. So what can you do? What do you do?

You face war alone because they want you to dim your light, due to their darkness within, mostly jealousy that cannot comprehend your light. They cannot comprehend your light so they will hinder your flight. So, you have to war alone for a season.

You wonder what you did so bad to deserve this, but this is where your strength comes from. This is what shapes your character and establishes while determining if you have blind faith in God.

The worLd will tell you to think, believe, and do one thing, however, the Father will tell you another.

Where do you fit in on the spectrum? Are you compromised towards the kingdom of God, or are you complicit with what God has called you to do?

You are more than likely in poverty or borderline, as this worLd accepts its own; and you are in this worLd, not of it, so it spits you out.

You may have children who cannot afford to see you cry because they need your strength to be happy, when you have gone two years without water and electricity.

Your babies need to see you maintain your smile and happiness throughout this because if the outside worLd sees your child upset due to your circumstances, they won't help you or your children. They are not designed to help a chosen vessel in this situation, because they cannot understand it. Being Chosen is not for the weak.

Instead, they will destroy your family and take your children away from you. You are now vulnerable to them, and their darkness sees you as their prey.

So, you have to learn to never complain, to find positives in the negative situations, wear a smile and be happy. But how?

How? You do not look at the storm, you focus on God and allow him to correctively change you from the inside out. You lay your burdens down in the courts of heaven at the feet of the Lord. Then after you have suffered a little will he release his joy upon you. It is his joy that causes you to smile through the struggle. It is his joy that provides you peace through the struggle. And it is his joy that causes you to not look like the struggle you have been battling for years. It is the Joy of the Lord that people around you see on and within you that causes them to hate you, and attempt to snuff it out.

They have happiness, which is a temporary emotion and conditional, which can change at any moment. However, Joy is a fruit of the spirit that one cannot just grab or get. Joy is a spirit that one must accept like every other spirit. Joy can be accepted like every other spirit, the only exception is with accepting the spirit of Joy is one cannot receive or accept the Joy of the Lord apart from his ways, his will, his commandments, and his laws. You have to accept and follow all to experience the Joy of the Lord.

This process teaches you to do things without complaining - Philippians 2:14 KJV. It teaches you the humility of the Savior -Philippians 2:5-8 KJV as he became humble and obedient even in his death; as we should be as we are dying to our flesh and the worLd. It brings forth perseverance, hope, character- Romans 5:3-5 KJV, and strength 1 Peter 5:10 KJV.

Let's be real, it is much easier accepting the spirit of anger. However, for a chosen, the spirit of anger which is wrapped in the spirit of unforgiveness will cost you everything; including everything the Kingdom of the Lord has promised you and has to offer you.

I once allowed the worLd to see me fall apart after my oldest daughter was molested by my parents, and my son was stolen from me. They didn't help me. They, the system, Satan's matrix, laughed, mocked, and preyed upon me.

So, I learned to take the battles and see them for what they are which are:

A. A test from Satan that God has allowed; Job for example, Satan asked God's permission to test Job's love for God, so God took away Job's hedge of protection Job 1:10 KJV and allowed Satan to afflict Job, commanding that Satan could do all but kill Job. Job was not perfect, he complained, cursed the day he was born, questioned his purpose for living if *he were to feel such agony, but he never turned away from God. He was rebuked in the end for wrongfully speaking but he was blessed double for his trouble, after suffering a little while. Or,*

B. *A test from God to test our commitment to him, and to show us our strength and how far we have come. It is through the test that you get your recognition from God, and from yourself; Especially when you pass the test, because you did what most people cannot. Further, the testing proves to Satan that he is not stronger than the Messiah, and he will forever fail at testing those who choose and put the Lord first.*

When the Father had me read Job, I thought prior to reading Job that God is just revealing to me I am in or just coming out of my Job season, and there will be double blessings for the troubling suffering for a little caused me; however, God gave me the eyes to see so much more than that.

Job 1.5 explains that Job intercedes for his children by petitioning the courts of heaven to forgive his children of their shortcomings; as he has witnessed them sinning. - This shows the example of what parents are supposed to do when their children are misbehaving. Yes, correct them, but you petition the courts of heaven with your burdens regarding your children and break the chains of sin off of them if they can be broken. If they cannot be broken, you

bridge the gap with petitioning the courts of heaven until
God moves in that situation.

1.6 Angels(the sons of God) present themselves before God,
and Satan appeared in front of both of them- This make it
clear that even Satan deceives his followers in believing
that there is no God when here he presents himself in
front of his father and siblings (Satan is an angel if you
did not know. The devil is just a spirit he embodied once
he was casted out and fell from heaven). This is why angel
numbers are demonic. No where in the bible does it direct
us to look towards angel numbers, nor does it state which
angel is behind angel numbers. There is no clarity in or
behind the root of angel numbers, and where there is no
clarity there is confusion. Satan is the art of confusion,
thus the angel behind the angel numbers is fallen angel
Satan. Satan deceiving his followers not to believe in his
Father (The Most High God) is just an act of rebellion, a
child against their parent. That is why it says mother will
be against daughter, father against son, brother against
sister (Luke 12:53); it started first with Satan and his
father, and Satan with his siblings.

1.7 Satan admits here he is walking the earth. - What isn't
said is understood, Satan has admitted to the Father and
his siblings that he is roaming the earth seeking whom in
which he can devour. Satan is always looking for a way
in, a way to catch you slipping, a way to pull you deeper
in sin.

1.8 Establishes that a test is about to go forth. God knew Satan was looking for someone to pull deeper into sin, so God offered Job. God knew Job needed to go through a transformation, so he offered Job to be tested for the sake of God's glory.

1.9 Satan is aware of the protection God has over those who fear and keep his commandments, so he asserts that Job is only faithful to God because of the protection God has over Job. - Satan's attacks had little to no effect over Job so he complained that Job's loyalty to God was solely due to the protection God provided Job. Satan does the same with us.

1.10 Satan acknowledges the hedge of protection, and that the hedge of protection is preventing him from truly afflicting Job. - The same goes for us, when we are in the season of elevation not of testing we may be scarred, but the scars will only scratch the surface of us, they will not be deep enough to cause any real pain. Yes within the season of elevation you will still have tests, however, in the stripping seasons the tests are far more painful and crucial than just being in the elevation season. The elevation season comes after the stripping season. - Satan knows that he is limited in what he can do to us, and if you are a true believer he will have to go to God and ask him to remove the hedge. However, if you are lukewarm, he can throw a pebble himself in your path and that will pull you away from God so he can throw stronger darts at you to destroy you.

1.11 Satan sends a petition to God asking him to remove the hedge of protection, claiming that once it is removed Job will surely curse God. - I do not know Job's history, however, I know those around him were sinners and Job interceded daily for them, so Satan more than likely assumed Job would fold as those around him did. - Satan knows our bloodline so he knows the areas to attack when God removes the hedge.

1.12 God removes the hedge and informs Satan that he could do all he wanted with Job's possessions but do not touch a hair on his head. - This establishes that God gives Satan permission to test us. God allowed Satan to remove the carnal and worldly things from Job. Satan can only do what God allows him to do, with his rebellious behind.

1.13-19 Job's children, cattle(that brought forth meat, milk, eggs, fiber for clothing, etc), servants were all killed or taken away. This test came all at once not in waves; it flooded in all at once.

1.20-21 Job worshiped and acknowledged that it was God that gave him those things and it was God that could take it away when he sees fit. - This also signifies which says the wage for sin is death; Job interceded for his sinful children daily.- See Satan thinks he has the power not realizing that God is using him to elevate his chosen and *using him to remove the things that no longer serve his chosen. God was removing what no longer served Job.*

2.3 Shows Satan will attempt to destroy you without cause (a covenant or agreement) to do so for the sole reason that you believe in God. - When a person is free from sin and fully surrendered to God Satan does not have a cause to offend them. On the other hand, when a person is deep in sin, or is scratching the surface of sin this forges a covenant and agreement with Satan, thus giving him cause to work to destroy you.

2.4 Selfish and unsatisfied Satan cried to the Father that the material things did not matter to Job. Thus, requested if God would allow him to touch the hair on Jobs head.

2.5 God gave Job over to Satan, but commanded that Satan not kill him. -This process here builds strength and separates the tares from the weeds. Many people fall away from God here, because there was no break in between the tests. The test just went from disaster to catastrophe in less than three months more than likely.

2.9 Job's wife urges him to curse God and die. She is sinning thus no longer serves Job. The wage of sin is death, Job's wife no longer serves him, and Satan has not placed his spirit in her through her yielding to him and began using her to attack Job.

3 Job curses the day he was born, however he still refuses to curse God. Job feels as if it would have been better if he were never born than to have the current life he had.

This book of Job is the process of the stripping God brings his chosen through in order to adopt us as his own. You have to be stripped of all the things that the worLd told you was proper and good, and the people who would hinder you from becoming the vessel God called and appointed you to be prior to you being formed in your mother's belly.

Job had to be stripped of his dignity to find Dinah. Dinah is the only daughter of Jacob/Israel, and the sister of the 12 tribes of Israel. Dinah was raped and stripped of her virtue as she was no longer a virgin. She lost her virginity before marriage in a violent manner, due to her father's disobedience towards God.

Job had to be stripped and molded into the man that she needed, and vice versa. For those with a marriage promise, you too will be stripped of what the worLd groomed you to believe and act as, and be remade into who God has called you to be; so you can properly execute the will of God. This includes a God ordained marriage. The marriage is not about you, it is about the work God has called you and your spouse to do together for his kingdom. You two will just be blessed in the process of your union as you complete God's will for your union.

Again, Satan thinks he is working to prove to his father that he can turn God's people away from him, but he has no idea that he is being used to position God's called, and God's chosen. We have to go through all the fruits of the spirit, and the fire in order to gain the wisdom, patience, joy, strength, and amour for the Lord. We have to pick up our cross.

I went from complaining and being a victim to seeing the truth and riding the waves, not drowning in them. Yes I still have my moments where I am like, "I am so tired of this bro, I just want this to be over." But again, they are just moments, when the moment passes I like, bye Satan, or get thee behind me Satan!

I have established my own philosophy, and now when the road ahead of me is filled with burning coals and a fiery road, I take off my shoes and walk bare foot across my path.

He that is in me is greater than he that is in the worLd. 1 John 4:4 KJV. No weapon formed against me shall prosper Isaiah 54:17 KJV. I no longer fear the arrow that flies at noon day or the noisome pestilence Psalm 91 KJV.

Let's go boy!!!!Let's get it!!! I have on the full amour of God, you can't kill me. I am protected as long as I stay in the will of the Almighty.

Your weapons may form and may even leave a scar, whether they be visible or invisible, BUT THEY WILL NOT PROSPER!

Being with low level men forces you to operate in masculine energy. Thus, pushes you to live through the spirit of Jezebel, while the low level man is weak, operating through the spirit of Ahab. In these relationships you will begin to look like what you are going through; and I did. I became ugly. My hair looked strained, I was overweight out of nowhere, and my beauty was diminishing. The Ahab was an energy vampire, and he was stealing my essence; although he was ugly too, in my case.

Papa, what is it to have full completeness in self while waiting for the promises you promised us? How is this obtained? - By allowing the spirit of God to change your flaws in the wait of God's promises. You focus on the self changes not the promise.

Okay, But what is full completeness outside of not being embarrassed, ashamed, having low self-esteem? These are just spirits, what is full completeness?

Not perfect, but complete. Completion is not perfection, as no one will ever be perfect outside of Yeshua. Complete yourself and share your completeness with others. Overcome and not be ashamed. Have a strong mind and resistance towards sin.

This starts with knowing who you are. Call out your flaws and your strengths. Make a flaw and strength analysis. Coming into agreement and accepting who you are is the first step to completeness.

You have to like yourself in order to be complete, and the things you do not like about yourself you fix, change, or rearrange, by coming out of agreement with it.

I am not combative - how do I make this saying a reality?

So, instead of saying I am combative you state, "I am not combative, I do however operate out of the spirit of combativeness."

Where does combativeness stem from?

Jezebel. This is why you are friends with the manipulator, because Jezebel is also a manipulator. Birds have more than one feather that flocks to them. These are the feathers of Jezebel, Baal, Poseidon, Pharoah, Harmanee, etc.

What are the feathers of demons, and what spirits do they bring?

What god brings low self esteem? This is the curse that comes with coming into agreement with this demonic god.

Come out of agreement, I rebuke, I bind (Matthew 18:18 kjv), I cast out, I denounce, I renounce.

When temptation knocks, loyalty should answer.

Temptation to complain about a situation, trusting God is the loyalty, etc.

This is why you should be complete in self before entering into any relationship.

I hear about and see many people getting pulled into Efi religion, or Hoodoo, and other spiritual religions away from and against the Most High God. They label this religion the religion of their ancestors and they "tap" into that, believing this is the true God of their family. The sad part is that this is not a wake up call to show where a person has come from, this is a guide to show a person where their lineage has fallen into sin and covenant outside the one true and living God Yeshua.

When someone makes a covenant with Satan it intertwines the entire bloodline. The bloodline becomes the home to many demonic spirits, so no they will not want to leave, they too will visit the children of the third and the fourth generation to continue their hold on the bloodline.

One is not supposed to continue the generational curse, they are supposed to see the where and the what caused the generational curse with Satan and break that chain, not continue it.

Knowing your family practiced other religions does not mean this is your heritage, that is a strong delusion from Satan. It means that your family pulled away from God here, and this was an entry point of Satan on your bloodline. Thus you need to come out of agreement with it and break the next generations out of bondage with demonic covenants. Now everyone in your family will not want to break the chains with you as they will continue the bloodline curses, so the generation that will be broken will come from you, their lineage will continue the curse until someone from their family breaks it, if ever. You will more than likely be called a part and separated from all the family that continues this curse, they are more than likely your enemies.

This not only proves the Bible to not only be our history, but to be fact as it tells us the nation began whoring after other gods- Judges 2:17 kjv, and were scattered - Deuteronomy 28 kjv.

The slave ships/trade that the Israelite so-called "Black" people went through, where they were stolen from their homes and places with other tribes who did not speak the same language, was nothing more than an example of us being scattered, for whoring after other gods.

The same thing goes for the deportation of the Israelite so-called "Hispanic" people. They are being scattered. All tribes of the Israelites will go through this until we come from under and out of Edomite lands, customs, beliefs, holidays, everything, and turn back to the true way of God.

This way of living, thinking, behaving, eating, being treating, etc., is not what our True God had planned for us? Why are we settling? Stop settling? Be okay with being alone to seek God. Be okay with losing those who choose bondage and Satan. In order for a man to lead the orchestra, he must first turn his back towards the crowd - Author Unknown.

This is why God told us to inhabit the land but to not do what the natives do - Leviticus 18:3-4 kjv

Lately there has been chatter about certain people using the blood of others to keep their "youthful" appearance. This in itself should conclude that the vampire talk is not fake but very real.

There are actual people who drink the blood of other people and use demonic sorcery to gain speed, vanishing powers, the ability to levitate as the so-called vampire does.

This is not a myth or a fairytale. This is the actual demonic manifestation and possession seen in movies. At this point the demon has full control over said persons. You probably rarely have a conversation with the person. The entire time you believe you have been speaking to and building a relationship with the person but you have been building with the demon(s) that inhabits and have fully taken over that person. It is truly scary.

People come to the end of themselves and their worLdly beliefs and want God to dispose of the other nations that have oppressed them and their families for years, but they (we) don't believe we are better than these nations Deuteronomy 7:17 KJV.

 We do not believe we are better than the other nations within our hearts, because

1. We do not stick together
2. We judge our own as the other nations judge and see us; as thugs, niggas, bitches, criminals, lazy, whores, angry, untrustworthy. (If you think people who are melanated are like this, how do you see the Messiah who also looks like this, and how will you see him when he returns looking like this?)
3. We do not support business in our own neighborhood, we tear them down.
4. We do not uplift each other and support each other's businesses; we gate-keep secrets to success and spend our money with the other nations keeping them rich, which helps them continue to oppress us.
5. We make movies displaying our kind as horrible people, we pay money to see these movies and we say word curses such as this type of person "ain't shit," or this type of person is "always mad, bitter, gold digging and angry."

6. *We help the other nations keep us oppressed and in bondage. This shows in our hearts we do not believe we are better than the other nations. The list goes on.*

We want status when we don't believe we are good enough and or we do not walk in the status we want or that we were called to be in. We do not teach our children or the children around us the commands of God, the way to break generational curse and the way to war against the demons that form against us Duetoronomy 6:7 KJV. We teach the ways of the heathen and those who oppress us. How do we think we are better, and how can we expect God to deliver us when we refuse to be holier than thou? Holy only means set apart. Yes we are to be set apart, yes we are to be holier than thou.

We are a holy people, but we do not act holy. We do not value ourselves or things. We value other nations more than we do ourselves. This is self-hate, this includes hating others who look like us.

The only choice we have is to choose who we serve. Once that choice is made, we have no choice over what our God or god does. God will have you prophesying words and helping strangers. Satan (god) will put ideas of rage to confront someone then he will take over and murder this person, even if this was not your intent.

Yeshua has never left us spiritually; he has been living through his chosen for years. His chosen are sent forth to prepare those who have eyes to see and the ears to listen for his physical return.

What are you willing to die for? Will you die to your flesh and pick up your cross, or will you continue to be the best nigga and or bitch they push us to be and increase the "Black" stereotype they depict us to be in movies, around the worLd, to others in our tribe (Hispanics, Haitians, Native Americans, etc) and remain scattered and held in bondage.

Even if you have a fairly good life, a life with God being Holy will bring you a better life with blessings you would have never imagined; and with blessings you can pass to the next generation. We cannot protect our next generation when we are gone UNLESS we become Holy and teach them the way of the Messiah now. Our sword which is the word of the only living God is the only key to unlocking the chains of bondage, breaking the generational curses from our bloodlines, and securing our next generations freedom.

A good man leaveth an inheritance to his children's children, and the wealth of the sinner is laid up for the just- Proverbs 13:22 KJV.

I am not perfect. I am still a recovering sinner, and living in sin pushed me from waiting on the Lord and his blessing and my kingdom spouse to being mislead by false prophets and taking custody of grown aged bitch nigga boys. In the process I became a bitch, as I would argue and fight with bitch niggas. A lady does not fight with her voice or her fist, a true lady is God fearing and she fights in her war room with the words of God.

In my bitchy days I lived the number 229. I was living the 229 before I even knew the significance of the number 229 or that God spoke in numbers, or that each number had a meaning behind it.

I had to go through every aspect of 229 to get to 229 (I will make sense of this momentarily; watch God work through me). Yeshua had to become the curse(the sacrifice) to lift it.

A part of my curse was being blind to the fact that I was cursed. So, I had to operate through my curse in order to see that I was cursed to break said curse. I couldn't just leave my abusive husbands because I harbored abuse within me from childhood. Until I dealt with the abuse from my childhood it would always follow and or find me.

I remember living with a young lady, her daughter, and her parents; I had a three-year-old daughter who had been abused as I was, and I had the spirit of depression, and oppression within me. I went for a walk around her apartment complex in EastPoint GA, and I happened to turn around while walking and I saw a spirit that resembled my blood dad, but shorter following me. This was that spirit and generational curse of abuse following me.

Everywhere you go childhood traumas will follow you until you break the cycles of them. Even after you break them, they will still monitor you, looking for any shadow of doubt or doorway to re-enter your life and bloodline. We must remain vigilant and prayed up.

The spirit of abuse found me in friends, teachers, coworkers, neighbors, family members, and my first two husbands. I would have said enemies as well, but the aforementioned that worked against me were not my family, friends, etc, they were all my enemies to begin with.

I left my first husband soon after major physical abuse happened on his part, but I couldn't leave my second husband so easily after the physical abuse happened on his part.

The reason why I stated his part when referencing my past husband's abuse is to be fair. I fornicated with my first husband and his generational curse of abuse within relationships transferred to me, and I actually hit him first. The same thing applies to my second husband, I fornicated with him and not only did abusiveness transfer to me but a deeper level of new age witchcraft transferred over to me. I hit my second husband first as well. Both of my husbands had records of hitting women prior to me, however, I never had any record of hitting a male before them, because I never did.

One of my husband's fathers passed that generational curse of abusing women down to him , and the other one had a criminal record of abusing women prior to me. I had no idea of this record, but in my darkness, would me knowing he had a record even mattered? Probably not.

This abuse found within my partners was abuse from my bloodline. I had to operate through the curse within the cursed state to break it. Satan thought I was receiving what he wanted for me, but God was positioning me to go through all the drama I went through for me to break the curses off of my bloodline.

No, I did not have to go through the hard life and lessons I did to break the curses, but I was severely disobedient and I brought most of my hardships on myself. God used me without my knowledge. God was my silent partner.

To understand the number 229 I had to break down the Hebrew meaning of each number.

200 in the Hebrew alphabet is the 20th letter and it means Resh.

Resh- a person who is bent over; a poor person. resh stands for rash which means one who is poor.

There is a difference when describing a poor person and one who is in poverty.

A dalet is a poor person with a pittance, however, a poor person described as a rash has nothing and is in poverty.

The rash type of poor can be witnessed within Nathan the prophet's use of a parable to rebukeKing David after he disobeyed God, had an affair and married Batheshea. King David lived a poor life, his son raped his daughter (inscest) and his other son rebelled against him starting a civil war. 2 Samuel KJV.

A dalet, a dal- a poor person with a pittance(very small amount of money maybe even a paid wage)

A resh- is far from God; he entertains flagrant, evil thoughts, speaks negativity; He is beyond the level of having or not having money; He is spiritually bereft (deprived); he is the poorest of the poor.

There is no poor person, except he who is poor in knowledge.

Rash/Rasha is an evil person.

When a wicked person repents he becomes baal teshuvah which means master (baal) of return(teshuvah). When a person repents Resh no longer means Rasha- an evil person it becomes Rosh which means head.

Resh when referencing a person who is unrepented becomes Rasha. Rash is an evil person; one who is far from God; He is flagrant, has evil thoughts, speaks negatively; He is in poverty and poor; He is beyond the level of having and not having; he is spiritually bereft(the poorest of the poor).

Resh when referring to a person who has repented leaves from being Rasha and becomes Rosh. Rosh means head.

The symbol for Resh (ר) if drawn fully becomes (כ) which is 20 (Kaf/Keter), the numeric equal of Resh is Kaf x Kaf.

Resh at times poor and at times wicked, has the ability to teshuvah (Return). It can be awakened from its slumber (sleep/dream state) and repent.

Resh can be transformed into the rosh- the head of God's people.

To be poor is the tail; to be repented is the head (Deuteronomy 36:26 KJV)

Kaf the number 20 which means the palm of the hand. This references molding and shaping

Tet (u) the number 9 which means the power to create.

So, 229 is broken down to mean:

200(Resh) when repented- the beginning of a new phase/covenant, leadership, the head/crown; the ability to transition, breakdown and rebuild; a person of prominence ; a covering, authority; the head is the start of the body

- When unrepented- a wicked person; one who is beyond having or not having, evil thoughts, the lowest of the low; poor in spirit; you are the tail not the head and you lack the ability to lead, rebuild, and the covering of the Lord is not among you.

20(Kaf) - the palm of the hand; the ability to shape and influence; the ability to grasp, receive; symbolizes what one contains within their heart(a person with the spirit of the Lord within their heart will influence those around them to be and do good, and they will receive the will and knowledge of the Lord); containment; bending shaping, molding and spiritual faculty of the crown/ head(Resh)

- When a person is unrepented they will bend, be molded, and shaped to wickedness, and evil is what will be in their heart; thus they will influence and yield to evil.

9(Tet)- the power to create; life and death is in the power of the tongue(Proverbs 18:21 KJV); Potential becomes reality; the feminine concept representing the womb (9 months of pregnancy) the end of a pregnancy and the start of a new cycle; container of transformations; a container where things changes and transforms, bringing infinite into the finite; the need to move past, past success or failures and focus on new opportunities.

When un repented a person will speak death over their situation and will not bring the infinite into their finite situation. We do not have the power to manifest, as manifest is defined in Hebrew to make appear.

We cannot make anything appear as we are not God. We do however, have the ability to speak the blessings God has already ordained over our lives, or the curses found in Deuteronomy over lives, as Satan would have us live out; as life and death are in the power of our words. We can speak word blessings or word curses.

The infinite is God's unlimited nature which signifies the freedom we have once we surrender to him and his will. This freedom is a freedom not only from generational curses, but freedom from all limitations, because God is eternal, omnipresent, and omniscient with boundless knowledge, power, and presence within his possession. God is limitless in time, space, and every other attribute you can think of or imagine.

When one is wicked a person operates in a finite nature which is a nature of limitations, because they are outside the presence and will of God. They operate bound to curses within the boundary of the curses they are chained by. One who is wicked operates through finiteness because *they cannot understand God's infinite power. Thus they lean onto their own understanding and fall short every time.*

With the number 9 (Tet) there is an aspect of duality where one has the potential to make righteousness their reality and they equally have the potential to make evil their reality. The potential depends solely on which God/god they yield to and serve. It depends on whether a person yields to faith or yields to fear.

I had no clue I was a cursed person trapped in generational curses of trauma and sin. In order for me to see and have the veil removed, I had to become the very curses trying to destroy me, then God gave me a choice.

God couldn't provide me the choice prior to me going through the process of becoming the generational curses that oppressed me my entire life because I couldn't see nor did I believe I was a cursed person. I thought I was living for God while sinning, but I had a one way ticket to hell #hellbound.

Once I yielded to the curses that worked against me my entire life, I was able to distinguish between God's way and the way of the worLd. It was only then God gave me a choice to choose him or continue living for the worLd.

I had to break down the old me to transcend into infinite (the presence of God) from finite (the limitations of Satan).

The Heavenly Father is my solution, he is my Rock, and my constant. There is no wavering with my Lord.

God is the solid; the truth, apart from sin. In sin you will always see his hand working in my life separate from me as I was leading a life of sin. I walked a life where I was a solute; as you could clearly see I lived a life separate from God who is the solution to all matters of life. When I fully surrendered to God, I became solvent(a process where the solid was no longer seen separate from my life); I answered the call and the solid became mixed with my being, my spirit, my soul. Now when you see me you see him. When fear knocks faith answers. Prior to this when fear knocked it was fear that answered. False evidence appearing real.

The thing that saddens me the most now that I have come into God's light is not looking back at how lost I was, although I shake my head at times when I think back, it is when I look around and see how lost the people are around me. When I say around me I mean people I see when I travel, stream, do my day to day activities, etc.

I see melanated people both young and old walking with a handful of groceries, with a handful of children, to bus stops where they wait for public transportation to bring them to their next destination. Then I think about the grooming and conditioning process that "fallen heroes," who are men the worLd told us were heroes, but I think about how they conditioned us to believe that it was okay for us to slave ourselves by walking everywhere. They disguised this grooming process as boycotting. They made us believe that boycotting was hurting our oppressors when really it was hurting us, as it was not only causing us to be conditioned to strain and overwork our bodies, but it was establishing a mindset that this way of living was okay.

We were not supposed to boycott. They did not want us using or around them or their resources anyway. We were supposed to be separate from them as the Lord has told us many times.

Then you will have the brainwashed people say, "not everyone is meant to have cars and drive, some people are meant to walk." Then I challenge that and ask you, "where in the bible does it say this?" God says in John 10:10 KJV, "But the thief cometh not, but to steal, and to kill, and to destroy, I am come that they might have life, and have it more abundantly."

God intended for us to have abundance, not to be oppressed living in an impoverished state- state of mind, state of living, state of eating, state of education etc. Even if not every person wanted a car,-- but ask yourself, why wouldn't they want one if the abundance of the Lord was centered in their brain..- or they were fully surrendered to God, why wouldn't they want abundance..--?

A person does not go through the fruit of the spirit long suffering their entire life without experiencing the other fruits of the spirit Galatians 5:22 KJV.

With the Native Americans, Haitians, Hispanics(Cuba, Mexico, Columbia,etc), so called Black Americans coming together as the Israelites they/we all are, how is there lack? Where is the village? Matthew 12:25, Mark 3:25 KJV- A house divided CAN- NOT stand! We are failing a part. We are the Israelites, the Sons/daughters of Jacob/Israel, the descendants of Issac and Abraham, the heirs of the promise God gave Abraham, the heirs of abundance, prosperity, and most importantly, a God that will avenge us of our adversaries, fight wars that come up against us both seen and unseen, but we have to come out of Edom; the lands of our oppressors, and our enemies. We have to come back together as the Israelites remembering not only the visions and provisions that God has placed in our brains and life and bring it back to our Nation but our failures and shortcomings as well. We are not to erase our pains, past, triumphs, victories, traumas, wars, or battles, we are to bring them together within our nation, because this is what creates and tells our history, provides a blueprint and roadmap on how to recognize and overcome strongholds, bondage, but it is also iron; and iron sharpens iron- Proverbs 27:17 KJV.

Our history intertwined with the prophecies of God as told in the bible, will be the stories we raise our next generations up on, it will be the key to continuing a cycle of freedom. A cycle and or cycles where we live outside of Edom's control and back into the guidelines provided to us by our creator. These histories will be taught in our schools, schools that are segregated with our Nation and the promises given to our nation. Our children are not as successful under the teaching of the Edomite nation. The Edomite nation teaches according to the success of those they used as puppets to make their nation great or those who help shape their nation. The Edomite puppets and leaders are not us.

Nation against our God will not understand the teaching given to those fully surrendered to our Father because they are not like us. Just as we do not fully understand our roles, placements, and or existence under the teachings of the nation of Edom we are in today. This is because we are not of them, their god Satan is not our God Yeshua.

If you take a closer look at the system we send our children in you should see that most, not all but most of our Israelite children within the Edomite system are placed in IEP or mentally retarded classes. These are the children when fully surrendered to the will of the Most High God that will cause problems and will be threats to the demonic kingdom. These are the children that are

divergents and have failed the test within the school of
Edom. These tests are given to see who is a threat. Yes
they may look the same, but the way the child answers
the question provides clues into how the specific child
thinks. How the child thinks is how our oppressors
determine who will be a problem to their system. These
are the children that will be the objects of abuse, poverty,
gang activities, stealing, killing, fornication, etc. the most,
because Satan needs to keep these type of children in their
lowest forms, so he can not only control the things that
happen in their lives and their destinies, but also so he
can work to prevent these types of children for finding out
their strength, power, and who they really are.

There should never be a system that teaches kids that they
are not good, smart, or wise enough. Instead there should
be a system that breaks the chains around children falling
behind so they can be good, smart, and wise enough as the
other children around them.

However, I digress....

So, when it comes to looking at the Strong's Concordance
meaning of 229 in its totality it means Aletho- to speak
the truth, to be truthful. The origin from aleo, to grind or
grinding.

- Matthew 24:41 KJV- "Two women will be grinding
  grain together; one will be taken and the other left."

While in sin, God constantly called me to righteousness as the contents of my life reflected labor such as grinding at the mill; and the nothingness within my life carried the weight of death which is equivalent to the woman who was a sinner and was taken away when the Messiah returned.

Even if we separate 229 from 200, 20, and 9 and look at it as seeing the number 2 twice then nine it still describes the state my life was in compared to how it should have been.

The number two just as the number 9 has duality do it. When we look at the number 2 and its duality we should go back to Genesis 2:9 KJV. In Gen 2:9 God describes two sets of trees, the tree of life and the tree of the knowledge of good and evil. Here God informs Adam that he was free to eat from the tree of life without consequence, however he should not eat from the tree of the knowledge of good and evil, or it would surely bring death.

If we look at our lives in the state that it is in now we see the effects Adam and Eve eating from the tree of knowledge has played in our life. The knowledge of good and evil provides temptation. Have you ever seen the cartoon where the cat has an angel in his left ear and the devil in his right ear? Well that is the knowledge of good and evil. It wages obedience to God's will against the way of the worLd.

It provides the choice to choose God or Satan. Without the free will to choose which God we serve, eternal life was always guaranteed. Once Adam and Eve ate from the tree of knowledge of good and evil, death was added to the equation.

Then you have those who think Satan was just given us the choice to choose how we want to live versus it being laid out and picked for us. It is those people who fail to see the bigger picture. The bigger picture is that Satan did not want us to have the freedom to choose our own path, because he knows there is no such thing as a being having the ability to choose their own path, that is ridiculous.

Satan was jealous that he was sentenced to death and man made in the image of God was given eternal life. With his jealousy, Satan made it so not only he would be sentenced to death, but Adam and Eve, and those that followed him would be also. Then he sealed the illusion of being free to choose our own life by pushing his agenda of free will upon us.

Again, the only free will we have is to choose which God/god we serve. The visions in our heads do not come from us mere vessels, it comes from the God/god we choose to serve, and their will becomes manifest within our lives. Remember manifest means to appear.

Just think about it, those who say,: " I have a choice to choose life or death, I have a choice to choose love, I have a choice to choose equality," are the people who are:

1. *Homosexual- the spirit of sexual perversion, which includes rapists, pedophiles, prostitutes, sex trafficking, molestation, adultrey, animal sex (bestiality), masturbation, plant sex. Etc- all are abominations to God; Exodus 22:19 KJV, Leviticus 18 (the whole chapter), 18:22, 20:13, Deuteronomy 20:15-16, 27:21 KJV; It leads to curses and death;*

2. *Condone abortions (the murdering of babies)- in which God says, "even the person who hurts a woman with child and it causes the baby to depart from the woman will be punished."- This includes abortion and the doctors/nurses who performed them, abusive spouses, the woman herself, etc.- Exodus 21:22 KJV.*

3. *Say we should be treated as equals and not different when God told us we are set apart from all other nation- Leviticus 20:26 KJV; 1 Peter 2:9 KJV- we are a chosen race, a royal priesthood; Deuteronomy 7:6 KJV- the Israelites are chosen by God to be his treasured possession, holy(set a part) above all nations; Deuteronomy 18:9- We are not to learn the abominable ways of the other nations in the land we come into(live in).*

The people pushing these agendas are conditioning us to sin, rebel, become disobedient(which is rebellion and witchcraft 1Samuel 15:23 KJV), against the word and will of God. They are puppets of Satan.

Satan has many feathers that flock to his bird self. We have established the feather of having God's people live and settle with being impoverished:

Another feather is the feather that causes us into witchcraft via rebellion by living a life free to love backwards, murder babies, and erase the identity of the true Israelites which is erasing the covenant God made with us, by making us like everyone else. We are by our actions claiming to be gods and making idols of our own works and hands. #hellbound.

How many people do we know living like this? So many people are confused thinking they are living upright following God, but they are living lowly following Satan.

This is what Satan intended when he manipulated Adam and Eve to eat from the tree of knowledge of good and evil, he intended for God's chosen to forget who they were and live a cursed life just as he does. He does not want the best for anyone. His gifts are temporal, just a tool used to lure you in. Just look at those who follow him, look at their deaths, their falls from grace, their treatment towards others, etc. Even the ones who received success by following Satan, then they decide to go against Satan after living the hellish life of luxury they wanted, while the true followers of God were punished for the name of the God they chose to serve; the reward for leaving after receiving the benefits from hell (fame, remembrance after death, riches, etc.) is sickness (HIV, AIDS other health issues), defamement, and eventually death. The ones who are not defamed are the puppets still being used today to keep the Israelites groomed into believing an impoverished life.

So, the number two has duality both good and evil, and my life mirrored good works from a hidden root of evil; although I had no idea evil was embedded and hidden within me.

Genesis 4:6-7 KJV- Here God contends with Cain asking him why he is angered. God proceeds to tell Cain if he follows the will of God his offering will be accepted, but if he does not follow the will of God sin will come for him, but he must rule over it before it overtakes him.

We see here which tree Cain ate from between the tree of life and the tree of knowledge of good and evil; Cain chose the tree of knowledge as the tree of life would have never yielded to death as Cain did when he murdered his brother.

Thus with two there is a division and difference. A division between sin, oppression, living for the worLd, dividing, and abundance, building, blessings, and dying to oneself.

Two is meant to be good and bring forth a multiplication of things, not negative and bring forth division (multiplications opposite).

Look at Noah and the Ark. Noah brought two opposites of every creature God called him to bring into the Ark. These two opposites multiplied and made more of their kind.

A man and woman are opposites that come together under God's command and become one in marriage, then multiply.

God took one man and made two beings, which signifies his original plan for us all along, to build and expand his house.

Two on the negative side brings a pitched forked tongue, which is bearing false witness(lying), creating division between brethren, separating God's people from God until their untimely death.

The only time division is good is when it concludes to building and gathering which is multiplication, and not tearing down and isolation which is reducing and dividing.

This is what living in the worLd of Edom has done to the Israelites. Living and being a product of Edom has caused hatred, division and separation between Hispanics and the so-called Black man, between the Natives and Haitians and so forth and so on, when we are one nation. This is how you know the system we are living under is demonic and not the true intention of our Most High God.

Each group within the Israelite nation dividing their traumas, past wars, and battles, then bringing them together intertwined with the prophecies of God to enhance kingdom and vision is the good part of division as it will in the end lead to the multiplication of God's kingdom and provide written words on the TRUE history of the so-called Blacks, Hispanics, Native Americans, Haitians, etc from our perspective.

This is why I stress the importance of bringing willing Nations together under word. Two Nations, the Nation of Israel and the Nation of Islam coming together under one God; our God. All Nations Under One God.

Our stories are intertwined at some part within our teaching. Stop bashing and looking down on the Nation of Islam, and invite them to war with us.

1. The structure that the Nation Islam has is what the Nation of Israel lacks and will benefit from.
2. The remedy to break generational curses(poverty, illness, sexual perversion etc.) that the Nation of Israel has is what the Nation of Islam will benefit from and much more; vise versa.

I am not talking about the puppet individuals who represent the nation of Islam or Israel and are parts of secret societies, fraternities, or sororities. I am speaking to the true men and women of both nations who are ready and willing to fully surrender and serve the Most High God, Yeshua and the Holy Ghost. Together we are stronger but as you can see apart we have been robbed of our heritage, stripped of our nations, ripped from our roots, and forced to live as niggas and bitches under the laws of Edom and their Edomite Nation.

Even our musicians, that left long-lasting marks on troubled youth identify themselves as niggas, and their woman as bitches in most cases. They too, though they speak certain words of wisdom, were brainwashed into believing and or identifying with something less than who and what they are. They were meant to plant the seed, and the ones that followed were meant to water that same seed, and then there is us. We were meant to take that watered seed, pluck it up and run with it to produce more in better soil, conditions, mindsets, and knowledge.

Before you turn away from what I am saying look at Matthew 28:19-20 KJV- Go ye therefore, and teach ALL nations, baptizing them in the name of the Father, and of the Son, and of the Holy Ghost: Teaching them to observe all things whatsoever I have commanded you: and, lo, I am with you always, even unto the end of the worLd. Amen.

It is written in God's word. Tell ALL nations, teach ALL
nations. So The Nation of Islam, I employ you to join us,
under our God. Two Nations under One God. Bring your
history, your trauma, your experience with the god you
have served, your strength, your wisdom, your
togetherness. Keep your truths, so history and the
prophecy of God will be told. God said Ishmael will
become a great nation and Islam has. Forget the
westernized wrong teachings of who and what our God is
and let us seek and find truth together.

The Nation of Israel is the covenant chosen lineage of the
promised Messiah through Isaac, but when you stand
under our God with us, God will still bless you greatly.
God will take your nation as it stands under him to
greater levels than they are now both separate from the
nation of Israel and together with the nation of Israel.
This means that your Nation will not be in the shadow of
the Nation of Israel. It will be known that Israel is God's
chosen Nation, but God requested and extended an
invitation to ALL nations to learn then teach who he is,
that he may be with them until the end of the worLd.
Matthew 28:19-20 KJV.

When we look at a person we cannot see which person is
living righteous and which is in see, just as I could not see
that within myself. It is what's in the full contents of a
person's heart that determines which person will remain
and which will be taken when the Messiah returns. Just

*because a person's intention is good and does some good
things does not mean they will make it into heaven. One
has to be fully surrendered to God, not just partially.*

*Proverbs 23:7 KJV, "For as he thinketh in his heart, so is
he: Eat and drink saith he to thee; but his heart is not
with thee."*

*229- Two women shall be grinding at the mill, and just as
in the times of Noah the one woman remained and the
other was taken away and the other left; watch therefore:
for ye know not what hour your Lord doth come. -
Matthew 24-41-43 KJV*

*Do you know that in my stripping season where I was
being stripped from the things the worLd molded, groomed
and brainwashed me to believe I went through a year of
darkness. Darkness where I had no electricity, no water,
no heat, and a car that did not work. So, my children and
I would wake up in the A.M. and walk hours to businesses
to charge our electronics, to get heat, and for the children
to play. We would use the gas in the stove to warm us in
the daytime and to cook meals, and the fireplace to warm
us at night. I would buy multiple bottles of the Primo
water 14-gallon jugs to wash our clothes, dishes and
bodies in the sink and bathtub, where I would boil the
water on the gas stove for warm water.*

*One afternoon during our walking journey to
establishments, God placed it in my mental to go left this*

time instead of right. We had received an uber the previous night home from one of the establishments that we stayed at for hours (sun out to moon out), and he took us home in a route we were unaware of. The route was a shorter route than the route we normally took to the establishment the uber picked us up near. Normally when we left to walk the two hour walk to the establishment we would leave our neighborhood and go right onto the main road, but the route the uber took had us going left instead.

Pretty soon, we changed our route and began walking through neighborhoods versus main roads to get to our destination and it was shorter. Once we could no longer go to the establishment, we just went into the neighborhood and charged our things at the gazebo in the front of the sub division.

The point in this true story I am telling inside of the other true story I am telling is that during my stripping I was warring unknowingly.

You see, ten years ago, I had a son in a Florida hospital and he was human trafficked from the hospital and taken to the state of Washington. I have been fighting to get my son back, both double minded one foot with God and the other with Satan, and now fully surrendered to the will and command of God. Behind me you will see bones and broken chains of the generational curses and demons I broke and allowed God to kill off and out of my life and the life of my children.

While I was in the stripping I would ask God, "why am I going through this," and he would show and or tell because you are going through the fire to get to the calm water (Yeshua walked on water and calmed it) which is restoration. I believed him although I did not see it, as all I saw was darkness.

Moreover, when we decided to turn left to walk the route to the establishments, we went through a culdesac to eventually just going to the culdesac everyday. It was at the culdesac where we conquered the darkness for the day, where we got to a place where we had some victory. Even when God gave us a brief resolution where we rented a car we would stop going through the culdesac but I would see the name of the culdesac everywhere, on street names, on trucks, in different states, and I would question God, "why am I seeing this everywhere?"

Before God answered my question he brought me back to having to walk to the culdesac; he did this at least twice. I finally move from the area to a better temporal area and I forget about the culdesac to say the least.

I finally got my answer to my question of why do my children and I keep seeing and coming back to this culdesac in a way that is I had no choice but to believe it was of God.

The name of the culdesac that I walked to and saw its name on streets, trucks, and plants was called Evergreen.

Just as Georgia is the Peach State and Missouri is the "show me state," Washington State is the Evergreen state.

So, while I was being stripped I was also breaking generational curses and the curses set against my children and myself due to my disobedience and ignorance. One of the curses that came to me from disobedience was my son being stolen from me (read Deuteronomy 28 whole book then focus on Deut 28:41). As God was stripping me from what I was molded to believe, the curses that came with what I was molded to believe was falling off. It burdened me and my children to walk to Evergreen, but the walk to and through was symbolic to God telling me I was warring and coming against those with the spirit of Pharoah refusing to let my baby go. I left and had to come back twice to war as their witchcraft more than likely increased, but God said it is done.

Once I was out of the season of warring for my son, God revealed to me why he led me to go through Evergreen. It was for my son, to break the chains and cycles my disobedience to God caused to happen to him. God will use you to break your own cycles without your permission and knowledge. All the struggles and obstacles are for a reason. Your biggest mountain, the one causing you the most pain and stressed will be warred and moved without your knowledge as you increase your fatih in God-Matthew 17:20 KJV

Two women were grinding at the mill, the Messiah came back and one was taken while the other was left.

Two women are warring for my son, one is fully surrendered to God and the other is fully surrendered to witchcraft and Satan. Who do you think will win? Who do you think will be left, and who will be taken?

The number two is good when it causes multiplication but it is bad when it causes division. Two divided can not witness, as even God calls for two witnesses.

Every wise woman buildeth her house: but the foolish plucketh it down with her hands. He that walketh in his uprightness feareth the Lord: but he that is perverse in his ways despiseth him; In the mouth of the foolish is a rod of pride: but the lips of the wise shall preserve them.- Proverbs 14:1-3 KJV.

Which woman am I? Which woman have I become? What woman is she who is led by pride and foolishly refuses to release my son after God has warned her it is in her best interest to do so? What woman are you?

What man are you? A wise man leaveth an inheritance to his children's children: and the wealth of the sinner is laid up for the just(those fully surrendered to God)- Proverbs 13:22 KJV. Which man has my disobedience caused me to have? Which man did my former god Satan always bring to me? What man is ordained for me by the Most High God? What man are you?

A Ballad during my worLdly years: Ballad of a Recovering Sinner-

<u>Even the Strong Cries By: Cassandra Bell</u>

I am the prodigal child that will probably never return:

And in my absence instead of lessons it was me I truly learned:

I learned that the first man I loved, never really loved me at all:

Since I was born he abused me in hopes that I continue his cycle or outside it I would fall:

I learned from him, my father that I was damned in love:

I learned from my mother your children are worth sacrificing when its your wants you are placing above:

I learned from me that I would fail them, and I would walk in their shame:

I was different than how they raised me, I walked in the shadows of the lies they told to darken my name:

I was broken until I realized that, that was a mindset brainwashed in me:

I was peculiar outside of the stereotypes, no, I found that I was free:

You can only be free once you stop hoping for freedom and make freedom your reality:

Become free of those and things whom entrap and cage your mind both physical and mentally:

If Love were free and if it was free to love then I would love you outside the boundaries set for love no less:

When you break away from an oppressive society, you are free to be you spiritually and when you love, you love free, less stress:

If love were a picture I would place you in the center and carry you everywhere with me:

But the reality in living in freedom is not everyone understands what it means to be free:

So, when I told you cared or there was love there, it was never a lie:

I am strong enough to unlock the chains around your soul or the chains by your side:

I am strong enough to love you through it I am strong enough to shield you from the worLd when hatred attempts to pry:

God is my anchor, in him I am strong, but even the strong cries - Cassandra (C. Renea) Bell

Let's conquer the worLd together! Send me a screenshot of you giving this read a five star rating with your name and testimony and I will make a book publishing your testimony intertwining it with God's word and will as he gives it to me.

Send the email to: <u>*sandy.speaks100@myyahoo.com*</u>

Do not allow the shortcomings of your life to keep you from pushing through your hard times. God said, "you are more than a conquer through him that loves us,"- Romans 8:37 KJV.

No weapon formed against you shall prosper; and every tongue that shall rise against you in judgment thou shall condemn- Isaiah 54:17 KJV

Remain grounded in the word of God, and free from accusing others, blaming others. Then the witchcraft those targeting you have cast against you will not land on you; as you have given it no reason to land- Proverbs 26:2 KJV

Keep the commandments of God Israel, and follow the plans he has for your life, and no divination or witchcraft will come against you- Numbers 23:23 KJV

Always repent for all things you have done to sin against God. Do not allow Satan to trick you into believing that God won't forgive you, because if you stay in the state of sin your sin will find you out- Numbers 32:23 KJV

BEFORE I ANSWERED THE CALLED: LOST

/s/ Yours Truly, the Recovering Sinner.

www.ingramcontent.com/pod-product-compliance
Lightning Source LLC
Chambersburg PA
CBHW072154020426
42334CB00018B/2000